Elsa Cross

Also by Elsa Cross

Poetry
La dama de la torre (1972)
Tres poemas (1981)
Bacantes (1982)
Baniano (1986)
Canto malabar (1987)
Pasaje de fuego (1987)
El diván de Antar (1990)
Jaguar (1991)
Casuarinas (1992)
Moira (1993)
Poemas desde la India (1993)
Urracas (1995)
Cantáridas (1999)
Los sueños. Elegías. (2000)
Ultramar. Odas. (2002)
El vino de las cosas. Ditirambos. (2004)
Cuaderno de Amorgós (2007)
Bomarzo (2009)

Poetry — Selected editions
Espejo al sol. Poemas 1964-1981 (1989)
De lejos viene, de lejos va llegando (1999)
Espirales. Poemas escogidos 1965-1999 (2000)

Poetry in English translation:
Bacchantes and other poems (tr. John Oliver Simon) (2003)
Visions of the Child Râm (tr. Martha Black Jordan) (2004)
Visible y no / Seen and Unseen (tr. John Oliver Simon) (2008)

Essays
La realidad transfigurada. En torno a las ideas del joven Nietzsche. (1985)
Los dos jardines. Mística y erotismo en algunos poetas mexicanos (2003)

For children
El himno de las ranas, 1992 (poem)
Tía Chita y Jerónimo, 2006 (short story)

Elsa Cross

Selected Poems

translated by
Anamaría Crowe Serrano
Ruth Fainlight
Luis Ingelmo & Michael Smith
John Oliver Simon

edited by
Tony Frazer

Shearsman Books
Exeter

First published in in the United Kingdom in 2009 by
Shearsman Books Ltd
58 Velwell Road
Exeter EX4 4LD

www.shearsman.com

ISBN 978-1-905700-47-9
First Edition

Original poems copyright © Elsa Cross, 1982-2007.
Translations copyright
© Anamaría Crowe Serrano, 2009
© Ruth Fainlight, 2006
© John Oliver Simon, 1993, 2003, 2008, 2009
© Luis Ingelmo and Michael Smith, 2009
Introduction © Tony Frazer, 2009

The right of Elsa Cross to be identified as the author, and
Anamaría Crowe Serrano, Ruth Fainlight, John Oliver Simon, and
Luis Ingelmo & Michael Smith to be identified as the translators
of these poems has been asserted by them in accordance
with the Copyrights, Designs and Patents Act of 1988.
All rights reserved.

Cover painting 'Símbolos', copyright © Susana Sierra, 2008.

Contents

Introduction	7
Bacchantes	11
(tr. Luis Ingelmo & Michael Smith)	
from Banyan Tree	
Words	33
Name	34
Shape	35
Voice	36
Epiphany	37
A Tightrope Act	38
Wine	39
Dancing Shiva	40
(tr. Luis Ingelmo & Michael Smith)	
from Malabar Canto	
I	41
II	46
III	53
(tr. Luis Ingelmo & Michael Smith)	
from Poems from India	
The Watchman	58
Holi in Jaipur	59
(tr. Luis Ingelmo & Michael Smith)	
from Jaguar	
Jaguar	60
Palenque	63

In Xochicalco	64
Tenayuca	66
Malinalco	68
(tr. John Oliver Simon)	

Magpies	71
(tr. John Oliver Simon)	

Cantharides	77
(tr. Ruth Fainlight)	

from Dreams
Tattoos	85
Reflection in a Sphere	87
(tr. Anamaria Crowe Serrano)	

from Ultramar
Stones	89
(tr. Anamaria Crowe Serrano)	

from The Wine of Things
Dithyrambs	99
(tr. Luis Ingelmo & Michael Smith)	
Eolides	110
(tr. John Oliver Simon)	

from Notebook of Amorgos
The Islands	114
(tr. Luis Ingelmo & Michael Smith)	

Acknowledgements	124
The Translators	125

Introduction

Some twelve years ago, I found myself living in Mexico City, a fascinating, vibrant and enormous city, and one which I don't think I ever really came to grips with during an eighteen-month stay. A previous period in Latin America had already led me to read a good deal of poetry from Chile as well as classics of the 20th-century *vanguardia*, but Mexico remained almost a closed book, apart from the towering figure of Octavio Paz, and the mid-century genius of Xavier Villaurrutia—both familiar thanks to bilingual editions edited and translated by the indefatigable Eliot Weinberger. While in Mexico I hunted through bookshops wherever I went but, while these yielded some discoveries, the picture of contemporary Mexican poetry remained opaque. Some anthologies here and there helped, mostly from the USA, and also some pan-Latin American anthologies, but it later became abundantly clear—thanks largely to the *Reversible Monuments* anthology[1]—that there was an extraordinary amount of fine poetry being written in Mexico, and that women poets—of whom I had seen little trace in the Mexican bookshops—were in the very forefront of what appeared to be a major generation of writers in the wake of Paz. It would of course not be the first time that women poets had been less noticeable than their male counterparts, although here I am really referring to their visibility to an outsider: it is clear that, within Mexico, the women poets that I was now reading so avidly were receiving significant awards, were being translated, and were widely admired. Elsa Cross, the subject of this volume, won the Aguascalientes National Poetry Prize in 1989, the Jaime Sabines International Poetry Prize in 1992, and in 2007 shared the prestigious Xavier Villaurrutia Prize with Pura López-Colomé, a prize esteemed for the fact that the judges are themselves writers: it is thus an award from the

---

[1] *Reversible Monuments: Contemporary Mexican Poetry*, Eds. Mónica de la Torre & Michael Wiegers. Port Townsend, WA: Copper Canyon Press, 2002.

writer's peers, and, in Elsa Cross' case, it was in honour of a fine new collection from the excellent small press Aldus, *Cuaderno de Amorgós* (Notebook of Amorgos), from which the final poem in this volume has been drawn.

Born in 1946, Elsa Cross has a doctorate in Philosophy and teaches the Philosophy of Religion and Comparative Mythology at Mexico City's National Autonomous University. It might be too easy to draw connections between the author's professional career and her poetic career, but it is clear that the two interpenetrate to a significant degree. India, and its religions and myths, played a significant part in her work in the 1970s and 1980s, above all in the long poems *Baniano* (Banyan Tree) and *Canto malabar* (Malabar Canto—from which the first three sections are printed here). In her more recent work, Greece—both ancient and modern—appears and reappears, and throughout her career the shadow of Mexico's pre-Columbian past, with its startling myths and magnificent ruins, rises to the surface. The poems from *Jaguar*—a totemic animal for the Mesoamerican peoples—in this volume demonstrate this latter strain in her work. As with all fine poets, however, Elsa Cross' work is not *about* India, Greece, or ancient Mesoamerica: the poet meditates in a space created by these cultures and creates a new reality, a new myth, even, that has resonance for today. It is often a deeply metaphysical poetry, as befits a student and teacher of philosophy, but it is also a poetry of dazzling surfaces and imagery.

Readers used only to Anglo-American poetry will find much here that is strange at first sight, for contemporary Hispanic poetry has a heritage that is quite dissimilar to the Anglo-American, having its roots in symbolism and surrealism, and also a type of modernism that is subtly different from the classic Atlantic variety. Also, where many contemporary Anglo-American poets seem to distrust the grand gesture and the oracular voice—perhaps out of a misplaced embarrassment—modern Hispanic poets are frequently able to use these with great aplomb. Thus it is that Elsa Cross' poetry can interrogate reality from a skewed perspective that seems quite alien to one sitting in a chair in England, but it is an alien perspective that I find liberating, in the way that it gives one new eyes with which to see. For, despite the metaphysical nature of much of her work, Elsa Cross' work is rooted in an empirical reality, even when it appears to be loosening its ties to the world as we know it, and to be ascending into a mythic realm. Elsa Cross is a poet who takes wing, flies over our reality, looking down at the landscape one moment, surveying the clouds and infinity the next. This is indeed a poetry that can teach us how to see anew, and I firmly believe that it is one that we need.

My thanks go to Elsa Cross for her support of this project, and to the five translators who gave of their time to help make it come to fruition.

Tony Frazer
Exeter, 2009

BACCHANTES

Man! Ah, Ariadne!
He played his flute and music led his steps

                Apollinaire, *The Musician from Saint-Merry*

I

We submerged ourselves in the spring.
We left our bodies to the current
like straying sandbanks,
a land that falls away
carrying off the shore of bulrushes.
We flowed through its transparencies
and in the depth of its bed
our legs brushed against a soft moss.
Plants entwined our feet.
We felt the passing of those fish
that, by accident, so they said,
would cling amid the women's thighs.
And always a phrase in my ear
sounding its highest cadences at the edge.
Downstream we saw branches against the sky.
The sun sketched on our bodies
the shadow of leaves.
The breeze brought your scent.
We passed under a willow
and its branches held back by our hair
all that drive downriver.

II

Surrounded by hills like walls
the men were playing on the terraces.
Din of racing on the grass.
A purple blue in the air when the sun set.
The birds were becoming quiet.
The bats were erratically taking flight.
The men were keen to score in the game.
Their shouts reverberated amid the hills.
Ovation.
They raised you on their shoulders,
they carried you downhill to celebrate.
At every entrance of that village, a church.
The seven doors protected by the archangels,
                                          so they said.
And ours got drunk in the arcades of the square,
talking of heaven and hell
as places separated by two inches
inside the body.

III

Nothing of your blessed prestiges.
The women were anticipating your coming, like an advent,
and you arrived with marijuana in your pockets,
your hair messed up,
just out of who knows what escapades—
And you had some queries to answer
like to the Queen of Sheba.
You smiled to see them so devout,
your milk sisters,
and like Shiva in the Pine Wood
unfolding a great phallus
you seduced them right under their husbands' beards,
the ascetics.
And the women followed you.
No curse reached you,
O Smoker-of-Intoxicating-Herbs.
Above, mirror signals in the branches.
The tranquil earth, waiting,
like a day of great festivity.
And there the Concheros went
with their flutes and mournful drums,
their hawk-bells of dry seeds.
Dance of mirrors under the sun.
In the district of the Cross rockets thundered.
From the poles they had hung coloured flags.
The people drunk in the streets
were moving in staggering processions
on the point of falling on the uneven cobblestones.
At night sparklers,
your mirrors of smoke.
Rockets rumbling like gunshots.
People fond of fire.
In so many places we found

mouldy bullet cartridges,
gunpowder burns in the walls.
The children puffed at the toy windmills,
they puffed at the flowers
sending up their petals on the wind.
The women followed you.

IV

On the edge of the ravine we awaited the night.
Did not the Conquistadors run their eyes
over that valley at our feet?
Lights began to be switched on
and our minds were being switched off,
since the vigil opened its spider womb,
its white goddesses.
We satiated ourselves on wines and odours.
And every night an acid test,
like the Bards on deserted peaks
strenuously holding atrocious and divine
threats.
Not knowing if we would leave alive that tunnel,
that night turned toward nothingness.
We let the sweetest wines
slip down our throats.
We satiated ourselves on honeys.
And at the height of night
the unheard-of grace of your body.
The world closed over our heads,
lost itself in the rain.
We forgot to mind our children,
like Bacchantes,
we forgot our homes.
The rain was a fiesta on the mountain.
And who could predict his own fulmination?
Open transgression.
Such fright,
Such beauty creating an emptiness around
sucked us like the eye of a storm.
And you took to my delight.
We follow you in the descent to your caverns.
And in the depth there were only

legs of insects brushing our back,
butterfly wings.
And the fertile goddess
smothering us against her humid womb.
Lightning struck,
thunders rolled through the sky
from the crest of the hills to no one's spot.
We walked almost on air,
as though walking through a minefield.
And an explosion brought us so much glory.

V

From village to village with stained clothes,
hair to the wind,
we ate, O gods, your soma
mushrooms all covered in dirt.
We were under the volcano
watching life being destroyed.
Danger on all the roads.
We made fires out of dung
to drive such chill from our bones.
O, mother cows,
Our bed of dung.
The earth trembled.
That day the bulls killed men in the bullring.
And from high up
the sun was fire,
our bodies oblation,
prayer
those cicadas on the point of dying.
And those drops about to fall on the earth
I receive them.
From the height we looked at the valley
and you were asking for fruit.
The clefts in the mountain, the crevices
made the wind sing.
That day the swallows were returning
looking for their nests at the height of the crag.
We saw their signs.

VI

We emigrated to the woods
like ascetics,
to an extreme harshness.
And another madness seized those fleshless bodies,
the eyes widened,
the cheeks sunken.
She stretched the cord to breaking
Her mind flew like a bird.
It went to the top of trees
to wait the rising of the sun.
But she stayed below,
she united her dry body to those blossoming worlds.
Cold salt of dawn on the beak of the sparrows.
She saw hummingbirds, nameless butterflies like laces.
Furies of death nourished her.
She heard trumpets in the air,
she shouted until she was mute.
On the verge of killing,
on the verge of blinding herself.
And the sparrows crossed the sky as if it was nothing.
The world went on the same.
Only her mind wandered like a rat through nooks and crannies,
and raked the ashes in the chimney.
And then it soared.
It lost the face of time.
It made her walk through the walls of besieged cities,
it made her scream from a pyre,
it made her sing dressed in coarse sackcloths
or frequent wretched cafés under the Paris snow,
pianos stumbling in an out-of-tune waltz.
Bodies were consumed.
She shouted prophecies under the sun,
she heard psalms,

she cursed and her saliva dried up the plants,
her thought could fulminate.
And yet she saw those yellow birds,
migrated from the north.
They sang perched on a branch,
they made love.
And she was delirious, sleepless,
and inside her mind
another mind observed like an eye.
And she flew in search of her lover.

We became deer,
we crossed through the woods like arrows.

VII

We were open wounds.
Sensation confused.
Your voice invented registers in my hearing.
Your musks intoxicated me more than wine.
Pleasure lashed us.
Inexhaustible,
inebriated,
our bodies, the offering,
like fruits that women leave
on the beaches of the south and the sea carries away.
We were lost to the world.
We sketched boats in the air
and we went off in them.
All night long there fell for us
gifts from heaven,
the rain on the trees,
and those drops sprouting from the breast,
ah, our soma—
where did our bodies end?
which body was whose?
I felt my caress from your shoulder.
Your thoughts passed through my mind,
and where desires were joined
birds of fire emerged from the air.
I flowed inside you.
And who were you?
Only a shoal of bees,
water glistening like jewels.
Waves of sensation confused us,
sent us back to the shore.
Such a view of the sea to leave behind,
so many woods,
so much of your body.

To stretch a veil in flames on all forms—
that we lost seeing each other an instant too much,
on contesting your thigh, untimely.
Thus died the fish in their nets.

VIII

Your face was scratchy.
Under the market awnings
a green brilliance on your forehead.
Your eyes, emerged from what blaze,
from what sombre places,
saw without seeing the plates with food.
A green brilliance,
as already reflecting the trees,
now seeing the countryside beyond,
where you were expecting to find a certain plant.
We looked among volcanic stone,
to find purple flowers growing from the rock,
cacti of fine shape.
The whole land of black rocks.
We were walking poorly
and the evening was also growing dark.
We passed the night under an apple tree.
We sought all around the mountain, without gaps,
came back scratched.
We sought without finding,
in ruins of pyramids where you fell asleep,
devourer of mushrooms,
devourer of iguanas.
You entangled me in your sleep,
you made me crawl.
I stretched out my pointed tongue
to devour ants walking along your neck.
And your sweat smelled of maguey juice.

IX

Scorpions waylaid us,
white, shining on the worn-out floors.
We walked in silence
between broken banisters,
our footsteps echoing in the vault.
So much dust on the roads to return here.
Something wounded us.
Words came back to one's mouth.
Were we developing a taste for silence?
A long offering,
an involuntary propitiation;
were they bearing us fruit?
In the cloister
cobwebs against the light like mystical diagrams,
trees of red flowers, fireblazes.
We put away their seeds
and passion flowers we left to dry in the window
with their crowns of purple pistils
like thorns.
The wine brought all love to his Name.
Something opened a vulnerable point in our breast,
a delight strange to our ways.
And inebriated, at dawn,
singing a chant in the garden,
you found your hair covered in dew.

X

Climbers with their blue flowers
in the impunity of that day
without a single cloud over August.
Dead-thirsty,
running along a narrow road
with their hedging of pink spikes at their sides,
following in a quintet
the counterpoint of violas,
we were climbing the slope.
You uncorked the wine.
And we were careful not kill any lambs,
not to fall over a cliff by blinking once too often.
Guardian angels alerted us
just in time not to plough into the hill.
Pursued by whom were we running so?
Following whom?
Held up at night by troops in search of guerillas,
lit up by torches,
their weapons aimed at us.
And so many butterflies constellated on the windscreens.
Ah, your offerings.
You put jasmines into the wine.
The wine, inexhaustible, redder under the sun.
Or we drank by night nauseating liquors
in the brothels of the outskirts.
Unceasing celebration,
at the cost of so much of our life,
our faces so pale.
And the ineradicable smile,
since anywhere
he was reborn.
Boisterous, Delirious.
We drank musts from his mouth.

Our bodies burned.
Delaying one instant too much scorched us.
And who could stop us?
Who could stop
those plants climbing along the wall?

XI

Infatuation with time.
We let the day pass
like sellers of necklaces,
of birds of paradise,
of combs of bone.
The branches of the trees bent with the grackles
painting the air black with their chatter.
'And what do *you* think?'
Philosopher bird.
Infatuation with the day.
We let life pass
like seeing those animals
from dawn to dusk grazing along the hill,
or hearing the water descend among the stones.
Our posthumous sonatas.
We got lost as those birds
day and night among the branches,
leaping from inebriation
to the delirium that stocked the roads
with phosphorescent beasts
or made sparks pass like balls of fire.

XII

Beneath the palm roofs we looked at the sea,
cantankerous crabs among the rocks.
The wind stirred our hair
and whipped the palms on the roof.
The sea made us listen to it:
suppressing our voices
and it devoured the land leaving exposed
the moist, reddish roots of the palms.
Taste of salty water in the throat,
the eyes reddened,
and an intoxication growing toward the sand.
Only one's heart is heard.
Breath that comes and goes, like a wave.
I feel the sand clinging to your skin,
to your hair.
It comes and goes,
a crashing wave,
a crest of froth in the throat.
An undertow stops the heart,
stirs it
like small shells on the shore.
And something leads us to plunge deeper
into the night,
chasm,
echo at the bottom,
a coin you throw into the well
and is so slow to reach the water,
echo in the deep.
And in that echo, again, the crashing of the sea.
Meaningless syllables.
Heat in our bodies.

XIII

Intoxicated,
with one's sights set on something else,
oh fickle ones,
propitiating Manes of another lineage,
we satiate ourselves on beauty.
Inebriated,
we heard with our body,
we dictated strange modulations,
dissonances.
A drop fell
filtered through the stones,
honouring the unknown god.
Thence we looked at the world,
a door guarded by lions,
a conical tower open to the infinite,
and the drop falling,
pulsating our bodies,
a vibration of sistra.
A spiralling sea churned by fire.
Blue poison to my throat.
And the drop piercing the image of my god,
filling the senses with its music.
A pause opened up
absorbing us suddenly into silence.
The world stopped in the centre of an axis.
Crosses of fire around us.
Only an ascent,
nakedness.
Ten arms from your trunk bearing flames.
Your forehead like a sun.
Beams spiralling.
You dance
and around there is nothing but ashes.

I myself become ash,
I dance, I disappear.
And seized from your body,
transfixed,
hollow like a cane,
I am the bed of a river,
a force that unfurls like a wing,
a thread of quicksilver,
a breeze.
We spiral on high.
Circulation of light.
There is no breath.
We are flying in the silence,
in the open void.
We are inside the lightning.

XIV

No image,
nothing that may tell a course
but the drop filtering in the stone,
overflowing currents into which we plunged.
And what we perceived with open eyes
was loosened from the shore of waking
to flow through those transparencies.
Dissolution.
Offerings carried off by the wave.
And we are, descending, matter disintegrating,
stellar dust.
Our breath inseparable.
Our sap untouched.
Oblation.
Dissolution.
A river-arm that holds back
a mass of dry leaves,
bees destroyed amid flowers.
We are arms pierced by the wind,
hair undulating under water,
exposed bones.
We are only skulls,
skulls of glass, and inside,
galaxies, nebulas, stars spiralling.
A fistful of ashes,
skeletons at the bottom of the gorge,
a ghostly willow,
a soundless voice.

XV

I walk through the atrium.
All the ground covered with violet bellflowers.
The encounter excited my heart.
Inside the temple
the seven archangels painted on the walls.
The May afternoon bloomed.
The offerings to Mary
were drying in the triumphal arch.
Michael, sword in hand, guarded the doors.
But we weren't headed for the temple.
'*Tanto gentile e tanto onesta pare.*'
And when I turned around
the grace of Raphael? in your smile.
I walked among the tombs
until I met you under the jacarandas.
The brick boundary was covered in purple flowers.
An ambiguous smell.
Beneath the boundary the Swineherd shouted.
The grunts of the pigs reached our talk.
And it will give no name to your froths,
since poets are such gross liars.

1981

from *Banyan Tree*

WORDS

Dark dwelling of the senses,
prison and boundary
of what is given to us in silence.

Oh, words, may they still
string together
              your image scattered by them.

They reconcile their power to no avail,
since they won't bridge
the gap between speech
              and thought,
between thinking and rapt being.

They come by themselves and speak of the "white chamber".

Name

A dance without a body.
A movement is born from the void,
a sound
         from silence.
From sound your name,
which iridesces at an inflection
                             –a peacock's tail–,
which falls in a cascade,
which falls asleep on my shoulder
                             –a turtledove.

You answer through silence.
You reduce thought
              to the void,
and there where you razed all image
your name is renewed.

Form

Your body is the night
$\qquad$ descending towards me.
A desire for form.
$\qquad$ Explosion.
Spots of light arrange your profile
in the high and the low,
in the narrow and the wide,
in the lost,
in the forgotten,
in what's recovered.
And nothing's alien to your presence.

Voice

Your voice against the dusk.
The wind pushes
                over the windowpane
the branches of the tall oaks.

Your voice fills the space.
And there are no instruments
                      for your song.
Your voice sketches signs in the wind.

Night
skirts around in silence
                that core
where light still lingers
while your voice,
            your sole voice
erases the moment.

Epiphany

Sometimes you appear, and the moment I turn
to your image
               you vanish.
Where do you go?
Where do you hide
all that time you delay in returning?
You come in dreams
and when memory tries to capture you
                                 I wake up.
Your eyes remain only an instant.
And to recover them
all this toil, night and day.

A Tightrope Act

A rope over an abyss.
I go along it,
          walk with slow steps,
sway,
      halt.

And what if I fell?
And if I fell, what then?
                  Fall . . . where?
Where can I fall where you are not?

Wine

A word suffices,
          a shift of desire
to bring suddenly
            all this inebriation.
Wine that is distilled in the slowest of drops.
Nectar—
subtler than ether
        descends to the heart
and there
        the *spell*.

Intoxicated with God, my eyes.
Intoxicated my hands.

To fill the cup to the brim, they say.

Your face everywhere,
your inebriated gaze.

Dancing Shiva

Ants are crawling up the foot of your statue.
Spider webs plait your hair
to the world's circle,
                      an arch of fire.
All tangled,
        full of skulls,
you drink ants.

A drum in your right hand,
                        a leaping pleasure.
Its roar created the universe
which you hold
            on your palm
There too
the fire that destroys everything.
Ashes fly off
            where your dance is unleashed.

Night is lost
            in the eye of silence
from where words and creatures emanate.

Your step is halted in bronze.
You burn all memories backwards,
forwards all expectations.
And in the pure present
I simply am you
            you are to me.

The ends of the earth
at the tips of your tangled hair.

from *Malabar Canto*

*A dream breaks our fetters
and sinks us in the Father's lap.*

Novalis, Hymns to the Night

I

The whole evening yielded to the passage of wind.
The trees bent like bows
and an unforeseen arrow struck my heart.
I wandered along those paved roads
where so much life was built on your footsteps.
The wind raised dust storms in the middle of the fields,
unsettling those red birds,
wiping out camps of insects in the crevices.
The earth lays dust on my lips—its offering.
And my offering to the statues that guard the road?
Merely words?

I was by the banyan tree
that evening on which the cooing of the turtle-doves
made so much beauty unbearable.
Night was slowly entering your gardens.
I was beside the statue of Yama, Lord of Death,
riding his black buffalo while Savitri
argued to win back the life of her beloved.
So much beauty about to die.
I saw you for the last time there, from the banyan tree.
Though large, the wind had uprooted it,
and the fallen branches had taken root.

Where do dreams go when we wake?
Whispered silence, squandering of time—
death, undecided: a murmur that crosses through the pond.

Your arms encircle me in my dream.
Your arms dissolving into nothingness.
Like a tree uprooted from a dry soil.
And everywhere abundance, burgeoning lives.
Insects passing, bees buzzing,
your sweet taste choking me.

Without knowing it yet, immersed in your ecstasy
I awake, while you go sinking into silence,
as those layers of light about to be erased
still gleam out of their fading gold
before forsaking the mountain,
the pond, the river, the open fields.
Not knowing on which bank of dreams, I hear at once
'he left his body'—and the chants from afar.
Everything halts in your silence.
Your image within me, anointed like a statue,
your gaze turned toward the infinite.

Who awoke to what? Who was the dreamer?
Light opened time with a dark beam;
it played on the eyelids.
The full moon was shed over the fields.
And that water on the pillow like ambrosia,
for at the same time you fall asleep forever
I awaken with a sweet juice on my lips,
elated with a joy that glares over my head,
that lightens up through my back like eels.
Outside the full moon, lost songs.
Your eyes from the deep of an unceasing night.

*

At Yama's feet
my eyes are fixed on a spot.
Gaze goes inward

and the deeper it goes the more around it looks.
Mountains grow large:
sole solidity in so much dream.
Fires dance, the earth burns
and from the dance it lets fall colourful fruits,
clothes of dreams where your serpents nest,
oh Charmer.

You take in me the form of the Terrible One
three-headed God.
It is you who create me and sustain me,
you who destroy me.
You hide from my eyes, you reveal yourself,
and from your soundless lips
words keep sprouting and choke me;
your very form becomes those words
that only permit awareness to see
that it is you who throb,
who enjoy, who act, who know.

You radiate from me, airy blaze.
In me you kindle, in me you flare.
You take in me the form of the bee,
you intoxicate everything,
you dissolve in me—thus you fulfil me.
You buzz in my ears,
you fill me with your saps, ah Impatient One,
you devour the accruing honey.
Open lotus in my chest.
Birds that drink the moonlight.

You take in me the form of delight.
A flutter satiates you,
a voice barely brushing,
a caress immersed in water,
ah Wine-Server.

You are the root of all throbbing,
the breath that creates wind,
the joy that rises to my waist
and twists there.

You utter me, dictate me,
enforce a deceiving silence—
for words buzz by like bees.
Seed of fire between my lips, root-letters,
words that obscure the objects they name.
And you, the Well-versed,
lead the silence rising up through my back,
fluttering in my throat,
swell mute syllables that absorb to themselves
all that fluctuating matter
between name and meaning, between form and object,

you pierce the forehead's moon,
you rule from on high, assault, break,
saturate every atom in silence.
And I am within you, impassive.
My senses dissolve in this waveless sea,
words become quiet,
and one step further on the mind opens up
to the shock of its own annulment.
Your joy almost tangibly, ignites, throbs
with the intent of an eternal embrace.

*

Death faces day
if you depart,
if you settle on your own beauty
and your gaze, turned toward the void,
shines only like quicksilver,
unceasing for itself, absent all around;

if it glows for what it sees and I don't see.
Who married Death?
Who is bewildered by these turtle-doves?
Ceaseless the wind in the banyan.
It drops a scentless flower in my lap.

Your body dissolves into earth and ether.
Fire, air and water return to their source.
You fuse space in you, absorb time in you.
You assume your primordial form, an eternal body.
Night enters your gardens
and trees darken their own leaves.
Everything is your sombre countenance,
your gaze turned toward eternity.
And what is revealed from your face
is just one edge of an infinite diamond,
a sourceless bliss throbbing within and for itself.

Ecstasy assumes the form of your death.
Darts fix you in the darkness,
suspend you from the sky.
I pick up the fragments of night
as of the body of my dismembered god.
The Malabar lark is heard afar,
the air evaporates.
My eyes close to your forms,
your voice refines to a thread
and an uncertain dawn arrives, a tepid dawn
like an embrace slowly dissolving.

II

From the ruins of our own story
a god smiles with his eyes closed.
Doors so high, as in the palaces of Ur—
and amid walls
insects that chew the dried-up grass.
Night uncovered,
a night where I look for you at every turn.
And though I wake suddenly with sand in my mouth
I'm still fixed; myself a pale star,
they look at me, point at me
as if recognising Sirius in the desert.

Golden coasts, ivory coasts,
Malabar Coast,
              tower of dawn—
silent hills of another time
allow their din of crows to be heard.
A tulsi bush at every door.
Men who see the god everywhere
and where they mark forms on tree-trunk or rock
they erect altars, anoint, paint with saffron
a face protruding on the bark.
A pair of eyes, a round shape, is good enough.
And I, where shall I seek your form at every turn?

The encounter is deemed fate.
But this walking through which endless streets,
this waiting filled with what stories,
this night open to what course.
I defend my escape.
I build my exile at dawn.
Blurred story, if seen crossways.
Do I come from me through my own self to myself?
I look for your face
in the memory of your ruined houses.

From the stained walls a white smoke rises.
Gods that have come down to us
holding an oblation between their red teeth,
their eyelids anointed.
And in the instant in which pain turns to me
I just burst into laughter, for I know
the eyes that hide behind the mask—
but oblivion returns.
Present in everything
thus you also disappear.

I wander through bazaars at daybreak.
I arrive at the courtyard of a temple
and my feet are as white
as the recently washed flagstones.
With offerings in hand I see myself walking and prostrating.
They mark my forehead with holy powders,
ashes, as the day I was born.
They fill me with flowers, consecrate me.
I walk around the temple
and lose myself at a corner.

Ah, my secret name.
Your joy—oh Mother—your boundless pleasure
condenses and falls down,
turns into stone and grass,
into a child in the paddy fields,
into cranes flying through a dark sky,
a tiger appearing in the hills,
mottled orchids,
the very shape of my body,
the clinking of my bangles on the floor
if I surrender and you dance upon me.

My songs lose themselves.
I forget everything—

lushness, time, mountains.
I change the pace of my bare steps,
I let my black hair fall loose.
My songs are lost.
I reappear on a barge crossing the river
amid merchants and a flock of goats.
Bleatings against the dying evening.
What direction, I wonder, where do I come from?
I mutter truncated prayers
and I let myself go on without knowing the course.

*

Landscapes emerge from a mix of dreams.
You ride a horse on the sand, your head covered.
And I keep secrets, dress my waist in gold.
Soft timbers—sandalwood at your bed.
A sudden glow and then darkness,
moving silence.
Heads heaped against the wall
and the call to prayer.
I see your face
in the memory of your ruined houses.

Lost palaces with their gates of gold,
with their marbles,
with their dead.
Echo of footsteps toward the same chamber,
memories under the sandalwood canopy,
behind the lattice windows in half-light
—filigree on the stone, lace in shreds,
behind the screen of a veil on my face.

A pink shining on the circumflex walls.
Above the minarets the evening opens up
the very heart of the moment.

I see the sun setting on the stone.
Thus memory declines in a longing to set,
like one who sinks into his own nothingness
and is only a reflection of the eyeless vision,
a reverberation of tongueless voices,
a flare of consciousness . . .

The finest mesh of light
covers the voice from the minaret,
eagles fly over their nests on a pipal tree.
The very light you showed me with closed eyes
shining here in the open
amid lepers and beggars,
over quartered rams and the smell of blood
as over the pure marble of the mosque
when at their evening ablutions
men kneel down touching their own eyes
and hundreds of pigeons fly above the pond.

This space we inhabit,
in the open.
A ray lights up
your very substance in every shape.
Thus the incidence of sunlight on water.
Where are you leading me?
But what does it matter, if the body needs but
a shack of palm, a house on stilts.
Where are you leading me
stripped of my own body?

*

Temple amid ruins, intact
on the scorched skin of the earth.
From the rocky ground

goats will eat thin grey weeds.
A pensive old man looks after them.
Pilgrims sing as they walk uphill.
The wind waves in their banners.
The wind, the wind
carves friezes on the rock,
devastates the peaks of the mountains.

From desert to swamp,
from paddy field to orchard I go,
as from one thought to another in pursuit of you,
you who pervade everything,
you who cover everything
and also hide amid things.
The slope grows steep as carts pass by.
Precipices.
Thoughts dangling over you.
You're either the chasm or the peak.

And on the other side you offer yourself in those fields,
crucified on the grapevines,
exalted on the corn flower,
on the purple crest of the canes;
consecrated in the river,
as in those great festivities
the clay goddesses submerged—
only their attires remain floating
and the water is tinged by the red of their faces.

Made of a different clay,
thus you have dissolved in every place,
and lotuses in the water sprout from your traces,
the wind carries seeds,
the earth tinges with a reddish hue
clinging to my feet as I walk through Dehu.
Men of God enraptured by heaven.

They leave their trail everywhere,
on the hair of women tending their buffaloes,
in the copper vessels by the fountain,

in houses that extend from the earth,
adobe both on floor and walls,
where the same chant is heard
that arouses the meeting at Alandi.
Men of God who listen from their graves
with half-open eyes,
their bodies uncorrupted.
The chant is lost amid cymbals.
People say their prayers at the foot of a tree
tying colourful neckerchiefs to the branches.
And I am there without desires under its shade.

In every shrine,
in the sharing of offerings,
in the sacred water I bring to my forehead,
on the sacred land I touch with my forehead,
in the flower I am given,
the same chant.
In the fire of Shirdi.
Men of God who light up lamps in water,
who mill wheat amid the smoky walls
of a mosque in ruins.

And you look at me from the marble,
the stone or the gold in their statues.
You look at me out of the night.
Bhairava painted in black on the dark precinct.
A lamp sets your eyes shining,
black on the white enamel.
And from the depth of a mirror your eyes of water
springing from three vertices look at me,

oh Tryambaka.
Down below your form made of light.

In his thumb and index finger, the god joins time and eternity.

III

Immense cities of stone
left a coded history on their walls.
A river joins its waters in the evening
when the air seems to fall from a syllable.
Seagulls flying against the tide.
Taste of rust.
Cities that keep that history, ours.
Great spaces mute to our song.
A river shines under the twilight,
dresses its surface with golden leaves.

Ships far away.
Araucarias grow through the pathway.
A path of no return.
The wind tears some paper garlands.
White ribbons wriggle smoothly.
As I see with my eyes closed
beams of light rising from my body.
Elation—oblivion.
And there's no port blocked to your presence.
It reaches everything, pervades everything, lights up everything.

Alas, memories of you.
With sand sliding under my clothes,
sticking to my feet
amid violet jellyfish,
I look at a setting sun
as one who calls upon Death
amid the pointed leaves of the acanthus
and sees bits of marble shining
on the dry grass.
As one who summons Death.

And what of Death?
Small butterflies flying among the ruins.
There's no measure of time.
The seagulls are profiled along the coast.
A wave escapes by the shore.
I see water sinking into the sands,
and suddenly—a feeling of sand—
the awareness of the body dissolves in the water.
Infinite confines.
Unlimited possession—

And there's nothing else:
a few seagulls looking at the same spot.
The last sun on the horizon
polishes the surface of the waters
tapering to a dark vertex.
Points of intersection.
And time is left outside all angles
in which calculations and geometries
trace their signs.

*

Beaches to which I'll never return.
Uttered words—
do they hang in the air?
for about a lukewarm rain on the sand I say:
'May I be a drop of this rain on your shoulder,
a grain of this sand under your foot . . .'
and before dawn
you pull me from my safe dwelling
to where the night keeps closing up,
concave, a blue womb.

The sea in silence.
Scarcely an undulation, oscillation

of the ships that appear bright islands.
I look at the sea emerging from darkness,
coming away slowly from the heavens.
You pull me from the safe shore.
Come, you tell me in silence,
come closer, you tell me.
An island on the sea, unbound.
Land in itself and sailing.

Froth leaves necklaces around the throat of rocks.
Islands of black rock.
Terns nest in the porous walls.
A necklace of froth—and I see my own wreck.
Night comes and shuts off the shine on the water.
Come, you tell me.
With closed eyes, just the tumble of the sea.
Still very close
those beaches to which I will never return.
Very far away now.

*

With no boundary, no beach, no froth
you add the height of night to the sea.
Only depth in the horizon.
The sky, all sea.
An eye that sails broadening the waters.
Sounds plunge into the air.
Cries of froth against the tide.
Unfinished phrasing—
and the night sinks everything down again.

Eye of water   drown me
Mouth of wine   intoxicate me
Breath of life   dissolve me
Form of fire   scorch me

Hand of wind   scatter me
Wave of joy   destroy me
Fence of froth   bury me
My hair your waves.
My voice water crashing against the rocks.

Silence is murmur, mermaid or conch.
The whole sea contained
in a hole in my chest.
I touch its depth,
unbroken darkness.
Indistinct repose of all form—
Forked tongue.
Jaws of tiger.
Vivid flight of a bird.

Black light devouring our bodies.

*

From the sea, sacred in darkness,
you brush the waters of my sleep,
you utter a word that dies away
when I open my eyes.
You return me to where forms divide.
You separate the wave from the sea, from the wind the voice
with which I now repeat the same name,
your name on this shore
where your gifts are countless,
and your rigor, extreme.

It darkens with whiteness.
Dawn unbinds its clarity
in the distance.
Deserted bed.
The relief of froth darkens.

The sea, a watchman.
Whiteness if it reflects
a load of honey,
a load of sun,
heightness.

The sea, the sea, pillaging at its shores.
Sutures on the rock shine under the sun.
Daylight spreads out its citrus fruits
over white mantles,
dims its sailors' song on the horizon.
The sea leaves on the shore
its sponges of silica
under the crystal of the air.

And on the water,
where rays freeze in their own light,
I see you like a seed of fire.
Every wave leaves trails of silk against the sun.
Filaments of light on my eyelids.
Blindness before this light
whose flash your pupils return,
pools of fire.
A dark undertow stirs blue valves,
shattered mirrors on the shore.

Found signs.

from *Poems from India*

THE WATCHMAN

At the boundaries of the village
two eyes shine
from the orange rock.
Sticks of incense stuck
in a ground crack.

The eyes interrogate from the rock.

And the face watching itself in the mirror
doesn't know who inhabits it.

I live my own death,
I see myself doing, feeling,
I am wrapped in my own net.
I look at myself from above
                —like a watchman.

The eyes smeared with ointment
protect the village.

Soon
   —the voices say—
before days become shorter
and in the half-light that's now spreading its lassos
our hands dry off.

Holi in Jaipur

Day banishes omens:
kites flutter
over the pink palace.
The wind moans amid the lattices.
At the tip of the wing,
                we live just so.

Women are returning from the fountain
with their copper jugs.
The morning air
isolates their cries—
names,
        ants of light.

The coloured kites welcome the spring.
On the sheeted roof
pigeon legs telegraph.

At the tip of the wing,
the moment fills us with the taste of love
and the taste of fear—
the same fever for death
                or life.

from *Jaguar*

JAGUAR

I

Jaguar child.
                Serpent.
Jaws open,
eye widening.
Your pupil devours the sky:
night full of eyes.

The river carries away snails
that stick themselves to the rock
                        —underwater turquoise.
The sand seals their secrets.
Spiders between the stone.
Swarms of bees among the flowering
                            in the slime.

Night where the tigers go down to drink
silent as flash-floods.

Jaguar child,
the night squints in your eyes.
You sleep
when the sun shoots off its arrows
among the rubber trees
and kindles the monkey's coat.

II

Feather crest,
fire opening a line from the meadows.
The old man throws his jaguar teeth
like seeds
        in the ownerless land.

Coatimundi,
        river of clear stones.
Old man with bundles of branches
                on his shoulder,
with his staff of fire,
with his bundle of years.

He appears on the hill
scanning toward the north
                with his staff of command.
He mumbles spells,
        lizard's whistling.
Lords with offerings to the rain
take shape in the clouds.

Tempest,
        tumult over the trees.
No bird cries.
The monkeys cover their faces with their hands.

III

Jaguar man,
        boy,
sculptured mouth.
You stalk me by day,
                you catch me.
Your even teeth.
Your hands—
        unfasten my dress.
Jaguar eyes,
        yellow shining.

You appear everywhere.
You come out under the earth.
You steal your claws,
your fangs,
from the Lords of the Night.
You are sun in darkness.
You are warrior,
                you do battle.
Your skin is stained with stars;
your arms,
        color of cinnabar.

You take me into the night.
We go following tracks
                we don't even know where.
You run like agouti,
you listen like deer,
you sniff the air,
                nostrils of jaguar.
Yellow forehead.

I am the darkness where you appear.

Palenque

for Olivia and Andrés González Pages

Tall in the shadow,
clear in thick foliage—
          presences.
Their footprints followed a long, long road
(yellow princess among the corridors).

The stones
stopped by time
like little acid fruits between the teeth
    —sensation of water through their pores,
    shock of the wind—
come out of their silence.
Begonias destroy the stairways.
Trees lift above the lacy crests.

No temple is enough for the god,
no temple contains him.
Turned into air,
turned into stone,
he pulses strange fibers in the breast.

In Xochicalco

Cows grazing among the ruins.
The dry cornfield extends a yellow fence.
Walls of fog blur directions.
No flower opens.
Thorns catch in clothing
and the jaguar devours the heart.

Drizzle,
         precarious offering.
Droplets draw fleeting signs in puddles—
no more fleeting than the day
when we saw what we loved most
fall apart between our hands
               like an ancient urn.

We waded the fog like a river.
It surrounded the hills.
Only the peaks emerged like islands.

Purple,
ashy face of earth.
Voices like bats' wings
through the stone notches
where the hills meet,
where the wind cuts
          like an obsidian knife.

The black air widens.
The mist blinds us,
it closes around the temple.
The same mist wraps the heart.

Higher up,
>deeper under the earth,
wherever she goes who gathers souls,
she who scatters ashes.

Tenayuca

> *Flowered death has descended to earth,*
> *invented in the region of the color red,*
> *it already approaches us here ...*
> Axayacatl

The stern night
will close its fingers
over the blurred lavender of dusk.
Silhouettes of serpents
poke out uneven heads from the simple line.
Thus the equinox brought
a distinct fate to each person,
and for us
it was the coiled serpent lifting erect
and casting no shadow.
Autumn equinox.
Its silence like a fissure toward another life.

Now, while afternoon still fills the horizon,
while we can see
the red sun descend
                fecund with blood
facing the Pyramid,
while we still walk below this wall
                full of skulls,
now, we love each other.

The Lord of Death
passed by us without touching us.
The lightning flashed from his mirrors,
under his step the earth trembled.
Step of a dancer,
                troop of spectres.

His footsteps left ice in the throat,
dust on the dry blood,
debris on the mute bodies.
We heard his emissaries screeching.
Their fatal commerce split the air,
and the sun blazed over so much destruction.

Mounds, leaves unfolding autumn.
In the depth of exhausted memory,
taste of fear going away,
of fear leaving us
when we look at each other
before its cry silences our voices,
before its embrace separates us.

Out of such ruin
where terror swells the eyes
in loss or wounding
out of such ruin we rose.
Intact, we rose to love one another
while death sang at our side.

Mexico City
September 22, 1985

Malinalco

The cleft of time fell upon us.
We wanted to enter together the heart of the mountains,
the night spreading its jaguar pelt
                                    across the sky,
what was at our feet in another time—
the immense horizon opening...

(Shrine so cool, so dark.
Outside sun blinding.
Hills piled up like dead warriors.)

Time opened a crevice
huger than the rift in the mountains.
Parted us,
we bade farewell
               —before seeing it—
to the slope seeded with that flower,
Malinal-xochitl—

        princess abandoned there, in another time.
walking for days in the wind,
nights in the rain
              to get there.
In the ravine they planted a stake
                        next to the rain-swollen stream,
brought stones, made an altar.
Leaving her sleeping
by morning they fled away
more silent than mountain cat
                     or snake.

Such moisture
clothing the skirts of the hills with jade,

put bonfires out.
The sky, brown as drum-skin,
                    resounded.
Flowers humbled themselves under rain,
                    —flowers of malinal-li.

Others came later to chisel the high rock.
With stones they wished to imitate the sky,
with animals the day and night:
guardians of the shrine
of neither day nor night.
What happened within no one knows,
no one knows what words.
Facing the cleft of mountains
where the wind entered
to blow the conch for the final time.

Others later shattered the ears of the jaguar
with hammer-blows.
The gods broke like stems of grass,
were lost like beads rolling downhill.

Now, in this time,
as unlucky days return
I break my dreams like clay jars,
now that sky and earth hang out of chaos
and everything disintegrates.

At different times we crossed the threshold,
tongue of the serpent devouring us.
You follow the entourage of the sun.
You left my breast cut open.

From on high the white houses,
flowers overflowing fences.

I see myself there,
no larger than a bee.
My heart sings,
filling with immensity
                    in this new time.

1985–1988

Magpies

> *Your glance already drowns me*
> *in endless darkness*
>   Alí Chumacero

1

A vault into the void,
               long clamor.
Graffiti on the tunnel walls.

From dream to the visible real,
from the illusory visible
                 into another dream.

He said:
   "Don't call me now. When I come you won't be able
   to endure me, and you will wish me to go
   and I will not leave. And nothing of you will remain
   as it was."

2

An immense wingbeat
descends
            upon its own shadow.

The earth is cut like a page.

I inhabit the crack you open
                      beneath my feet,
I become the emptiness filling you,
you, who are the abyss.

3

Night emerges into consciousness
showing your harsh edges,
a sliver that sticks its sharpest note
                            into my side.

To hear the echo of your voice
I plunge in your depth
and wander there,
                  blind fish,
until I am back
open as a question,
transfixed,
drunk with inexistence.

4

Thought
goes out to meet your form,
tiny points.

Clouds of magpies rise
                from the train-tracks.
White towers glow in the dawn.

At the end of immeasurable time,
of immeasurable space,
thought grasps between its edges
                        only a flutter.

The magpies cross
the pale dawn of the mind.
They flare and dim
                in the black hall.

5

Mane of foam
            inflamed,
overflowing,
radiance of things never dreamed of before.
The wave recedes,
the ocean opens,
the foam raises its wings.

6

Things about to catch on fire
in the midst of their stillness.

In an instant
the eye exhausts all form
and returns to its void.

My breast like a cave.
Your fire which has devoured everything,
burning there,
            unconsumed.

7

A flock of thoughts rise
                into the air.
They scratch at my breast.
The shadows that cover me
                are no longer the same.

I look into the deep
              where your image is waiting.

Under what omen did you pull these strings?

8

Your breath

              a wing-brush
    dances free

      it unites both extremes
      initiates another round

Your voice

              hoarfrost

    breaks the surface
    like a geyser

9

I touch a stem
      and leaves emerge,
I touch a branch
and a fruit forms
        between my fingers.

Your voice returns.
We are paired likenesses
        inside the same breath.

10

Magpies on the wing,
             persisting sound,
bursting out
      as on holiday,
filaments fall from their flight.

The music steady on the metals.

Vertigo,

           the black wall.

11

Like words,
      o stubborn ones,
they cover again what was naked already,
they pile themselves up
upon the perfection
           of the unspoken.

12

Steely gangplank
back of a sleeping beast—
           the sea of thought.

Letters like bubbles
rise to the surface,
tiny creatures,
moss—
      over the skin of the Invisible one.

13

What's hidden,
            about to explode.

I enter your heart.

You fill me with your nothingness,
                      you devour me.

14

The wing
        brushes translucent edges,
shines in appearances.
The ocean pours on the shore.
Your darkness extends
            in my consciousness.

15

Nothing can touch me
            under your shadow,
beloved as a grave,
as a lap to lie on.

What light allows me to see your darkness?

Thought passes
        with closed wings.
The soul takes shelter
        under your shadow.

CANTHARIDES

> *by the Omphalos, wrapped in shadows...*
> Pindar

1

The red stone
      —blood of the serpent—
fades into day

light falls on the sanctuary

2

Among the ruins
dry cantharides
glinting husks
scald-scabs

traces of aloe
on the tongue

3

Serpent
    the one who knows and begets
    who conceals
    annihilates

to reach her
you must become a wind
penetrate rock fissures

be the fire's tongue
        arrow of the god

4

Where they broke
the holy amphorae
she hides herself

her words
        scattered stones

between muffled footsteps
and thorns
her fractured song

5

In her agile spirals
her green suffocations
her pleated silks
I breathe

I let the dust adhere to my ribs
the wind hiss between my teeth

in her Orphic circles
her geometric eyes
her serpentine embrace
I expire

6

Word
dry blood on the rock
               threads of a voice

palpitate on the tongue
approach and retreat
               explode
in a naked blaze

semen and light

7

Intermittent
        blows of a voice
combine and rear up
into a single silence

               —hurricane eye

8

Resonance the stones enclose

the echo
        tumbles
        like a landslide

tangles of buzzing bees
twitched threads

9

The shrill sound
hangs in the air
becomes a bellow
                bull-roarer
penetrates pavilion
                labyrinth—

a multicoloured vector.

10

From the open mouth
                as from a mask
syllables cascade
        a gush of sound—

eye of silence

11

Words knot the form
in their mesh

honeycomb
        humming

the dream of the nymphs
nourished by their sap

12

Stuttering tongue
ripples
        of syllables

tongue of fire

devoured by its own phrases

13

From her mouth to my ear
words

the web tears
what grasped now flows
toward the west's burn

14

It hums between the chinks

slides soft fingers along the neck
briefly touches the thigh

it is the sure needle
sharp whistle   arrow

15

It passes through strata
              of meaning
that humid sentence

    wine filtered from
              a closed pitcher

16

In exchange for one flower
              of immortality
among the tense nettles
she leaves the skin
              as pledge

the wind bevels
              her scales

17

And the thorny voice
holds in its dry sheath
an empty shape

curls on the tongue
              like a living word
circles the haunch
like a sibilant hiss
              like a flame

18

She unfurls her coils
rears up
        from the dust
friend of those who imitate
                her cadences
her new skin shines
            —oh Radiant One
a sure target for your arrows

19

She seeks out the angle
where the ray of sunlight
touches the eye's surface
and plays at reflection

her shackled tongue sleeps
feigns that it sleeps
stretches into its fullness
savours its own darkness

20

She casts an invisible snare
like a scent

curls into a circle
lets her echoes fall
to the crevice's depths

21

In tatters
        the careful weft
nothing left in the hands
fragments of sense
                skin-scraps

22

She enters the darkness

unborn words
between these rocks

23

Voice
     contained in the air
word
         suspended in voice
—and the word, from where?

they have already forgotten

24

It disappears
        into the light's centre

silence devours the words
like tiny insects
              cantharides

from *Los sueños*

TATTOOS

With its blackened heraldry,
its relentless downpours,
                    the city is dying.
Around the fountain
young people shoot up,
sleep on paving slabs
with runes drawn
                    on their shoulders.
Covered in graffiti,
the temple rises
beside the rubble from the bombing,
          letters like twisted plants
—oxide on the skin of shrubs.

At the far end, the double row of poplars,
                        their gothic ribs.
Verdiblack statues,
faces tattooed by mold.
Inside,
some paltry light against the stone,
                        empty crypts.

Cutting themselves off at the root,
retracing their steps towards the unforeseen
the worn paths,
                iron rust.
Undefinable heat.
Momentary flapping at the nape of his neck,
at his fingertips.

Flavours not chosen
                radiate inside.
Recurring phrases/
                serial waste.
And in his own flesh
an incomprehensible reply.

Cut into his stomach,
                like a ritual suicide?
An option of lamps deep down.
Discontinuous
                sardine coloured eyes
—and the intense blue ad on the wall.

Close-up
only on sweaty faces,
                twitching hands.
The perfect illusion shifts elsewhere,
                        oppressive.
A foreign dialect
with no wish to express
quite simply brings
                its clean edge.

Reflection in a Sphere

From its centre,
the sphere of a lamp
              inverts shapes,
    a point of escape:
metallic borders bend,
the window frame,
the purple rose bush
                slide towards emptiness.

Night accumulated on the walls.
With no words to mediate,
they suddenly sink into those chalices
     herb juices
              in the dark abrasion,
an intemperate climate.

Oh long kisses,
hand that travels a thigh
                like a beach,
the curl in the groin—
                (*oh summer body*).
    And thoughts pause
              in that flowering
    like insects.

At dawn the unknown place,
                purple flowers.
The lamp breaks its reflections,
just as the sun outside is already refracting
                      over surfaces.
Objects go by like a river:
voices demanding to be heard,

shapes keen to be seen
                    invade the mind.

Untouched,
conscience is a mirror:
                    the edge of a scale,
a blade brushing a wing in motion.

They go their separate ways
without looking back,
without asking each other their names.
And the no man's land,
the half-sky travelled in delirium
                    now non-existent,
already teeming with lowly traffic
                    in the street.

from *Ultramar*

STONES

I

On the threshold
of doors now non-existent,
in enclosures barely demarcated
under the full-on heat
and its alliances with insects and dust,
the image that was dreamt
or glimpsed perhaps
                        among those stones
is subdued by an unfathomable presence.

Escape closes off its paths.
Boundaries break.
And what gave thought its shape
                        becomes undone.

The touch of day
and the cloud of dreaming
                        longingly
skirt each other.
And deep down
              like a cloyed fish
lies consciousness.

Its intimate calm
              unbuckles into arborescent light,
the tongue racking itself in the silence

till the magnetized names
                        vibrate.

Phrases repeated on the threshold,
rhythms that segment like bark.

2

Every century fits
between that morning
                and the night, almost,
in which the city appeared
like a dawning of time.

The boundary transgressed now sees the other side—
noises steadily climb,
                as does the cloud of smog,
and the point of escape is lost in Heroes Square,
in the waitress standing at the door like a caryatid,
or in the round Attic moon
crossing the rooftops between the angles of antennae
                            and vertical planes—

The question "why here?"
is preempted by the pounding of a drill.
And the mind receives the visitation of the poet—
Dozing I see the half moon of his turban,
when the murmur
brings me back from the vaults of sleep,
and the scent of aniseed and damp tobacco
                          envelops me.

And the moon in my heart,
is almost a rim
            under the circle of shade—
a presence not present.

The dream to which I wake sheds
the shapes I've given it over time;
no colour in the retina,
                nothing depicts it now.
It seeps through skin and dissolves.

What stops the mind at the threshold?
—the mind asks of itself before its icon.

3

From a sudden silence
a perfume invades the room,
it freezes at the memory of a flower
                              slender and white,
turned towards twilight;
from the wonder come the words,
"Iris, Iris,
you who died at the gates of Persepolis".

The heat holds up a taut arch mid-way through the day.
The balcony awning blinds with its brightness.
Screeching accompanies
the youth who is painting his terrace—
                              and that eastern twang
dressing the songs with suspicious veils,
as if they were doing a tally
of the girls who waited behind the windows
between insect stings
and the recitation
of the Ninety nine Names of praise.

Objects fall,
            the scandal of ill-spoken tongues,
while beads of perspiration
slither down my back
            like electric jabs.
The brain follows anomalous circuits—
                            . . . the gates of Persepolis.

On the radio confused enumerations,
                          meteorological reports.
Through open windows, bodies fast asleep.

The heat draws its pincers closer, like a crab.

4

The sun lashes, naked, on marble.
Inscriptions
hide and light its messages:
letters like porticos,
triglyphs,
 vibrant propyleums—
and just where things collide with their names
veins open in the marble
 like entries to other dreams.

The temples of words come tumbling down,
meaning becomes
 an incongruous sketch,
a particle that marries with dust.

Complete darkness under the sun,
complete ignorance.

There are no signs of the route.
The god opens and closes destinies
just as the wind whips the shutters
 till they break.

The steps are repeated.
And the blind questions,
the stuttering,
the staggering,
the bird-like wonder—
 waiting for something.

Words fall
 like coins:
their reflection gleams on these stones
that existed here,

       before we did,
and will continue long after—
                  like the gods.

A transversal cut through meaning.
We look at the oracle, none the wiser.

Everything begins where we close our eyes.

5

In the whiteness of the atriums
mid-day refraction gleams like a shadow on the retina.
Any apparition can occur.
The laurels of Daphne —Laura—
point to the sky, fingers spread in horror.
And the god's reflection accumulates among those stones.

You can hear the east wind,
the metal of cowbells,
cicadas:
      the incipient polyphony of summer.

The sun opens out on skin,
surpasses dreams over the edge of a shimmer,
melts differences that by evening will again be apparent
      defining the ruggedness of land within its range
        or showing up chasms
              between things that feign similarity.

Dreams crumble away—
        like statues of gods?

Apparitions against that backdrop:
the whiteness of the *daphnes*
speaks of the shade dwindling
        among its long leaves.
And at night, where will clarity suggest itself?
A wave in the sea
      where the moon instils its desire?

6

> In memory of Jose Carlos Becerra
> *... en bas la mer aux flots amers*

Votive stelae
to open the path for the dead.
Beside the goddess
children appear carrying a sparrow,
a young girl offers —or receives— a small casket.

The body grasps from air the idea of flight—
right there under the stones where
                        unwinged geniuses lie.
Or someone looks from the cliffs
at the bitter, beautiful sea
                        of his own wreck.
The superimposed image
takes on the shapes, adjusts features,
rhythms,
        flickers
of what was glimpsed on that pale flight.
Its playful moves gleam
like flames on lamps up high.

If death and reality draw closer,
are the gods more human
                        or men more divine?

Dreams like prayers,
darts that are aimed
                        at an invisible target;
forms of passion,
of vision—
            footprints crossing.

7

Antinomies
in the confined space of consciousness.
Dreams and reality walk so as to meet,
and face each other
only perhaps beside death.

The sun rises.
Iridescent grasses among spider webs.
The wind carries away eucalyptus flowers—
confused bees buzz,
with their solid voice
they prop
the morning sun

            —radiance of the gods.
What shapes do they take
when they descend to embody these lights?

Someone touches them
and wants nothing but to die
            on the edge of the reflection,
overwhelmed by so much sea,
so much sun on the stones,
with his dream stuck like a splinter
            between his eyes.

And your beauty
            invisibly
shines along the path,
oh Radiant one,
      great before all things—

Is what radiates
      from the sun this morning
gods trapped in a form
or men trapped in a dream?

8

Under the shade of the palm tree,
on the banks of the dry lagoon
as much sediment gets superimposed
      on stones
as on the mind—
creatures of thought
    or desire,
   —who engenders them?
which all-fertile god germinates the tiniest impulse,
the most trivial fantasy,
    as he goes by,
and turns them
into dark or radiant beings,
whose beauty overwhelms?

They, who leap to Ida from Gargaros,
    or keep their immortal horses
    in ambrosia stables,
unfold in dreams,
free of thought or turbulence—
and whoever follows them
is dazzled,
blinded,
  stops bewildered,
returns
  to the point of departure.

9

A river of stones descends abruptly to the sea.
Fossilized corals
on the trail the donkeys take laden with oil.
The spring flowers
have now become small brittle suns—

A hint of light,
             white gulls.

Waves repeat their prayer in the god's ear.
The port is enveloped in its own silence.

More obstinate
             the silence of the heart,
sprawls on the sand
among the untidy shadows of twilight.
Desires become bright stones,
seeds devoured by birds,
or in the dark they spread their emptiness.

The moon flutters like an insect,
pulsates
         in spirals over the water
and flush with visible things,
in the fissure,
it grows towards a more confined
                    recess of consciousness.

Gulls say of the soul
things we don't understand.

from *The Wine of Things*

DITHYRAMBS

I

You who untie knots
bound the two ends.
In the circle of gold
where time
        devours itself
consciousness upside down
            halts its fall.
And on that impassable edge,
the unharmed leap,
    turned into a wing
           in the middle of the air,
begins another round.

You who bind knots
become light
    in the middle of a cleft,
become letters like frozen drops,
salts in the glass of time.
You prick conscience
        —blood-letting,
           remote epicentre—,
and between what you say
           and what I hear
a corridor of mirrors,
an erased contour,
    thickness.

2

For Verónica Volkow

Your shapes are engraved on the mountain,
on the moist edges of the stone
                          —cavities like armpits.
Your shapes stick to my bones.
I cease to exist,
you alone remain
          like jade on these slopes.

How much of you explodes in each leaf,
reverberates in the distance
where your light consumes all brilliance.

(Am I in your abyss
                  or do I surround it?)

I am reborn in the shade of the laurel,
in the cell of a circular temple
if you support
with your gigantic foot
                  the firmament.

Your shapes like a vertigo
absorb me,
        dissolve me.
They leave on my lips traces of aniseed.

And in the depth of the cliff
trees like gods,
            red cypresses.

3

In the patio of white mosaics
the arabesques draw limits to the eye,
their curves restrain
              your unbounded shadow.

Brilliance of salt,
the more
              light blinds
the more shadow rises
              beneath the overwhelmed pergola
or in the stone corollas
              beside the fountain.

Pale
    like your face
with more shadow in your eyes
              than you join under the sky,
night comes.

Your silence
conceals the words
              carved on the skin,
your voice draws out of them
harmonies that rhyme with death.

Pale night
in those branches where peacocks
              of light dance,
tails agitated
       by the wind that shakes
your cortege of shadows
              and sings in the ravine.

4

For Myriam Moscona

In the field of the known
you stretch out like roots
                        delicate fibres,
you touch with your purples and your greens
interweaving of neurons,
you sink in their holes
                      your recognisable forms.

Something spreads out like a wing
and you peep out
            —crafty bird.

At dusk the river muddles,
the water silvers various turns
and what it carries away wrecked
passes like an episode under the bridge.
Attention wanders,
                  contracts—
foam
    on the vain surface.

In meadows of asphodels
your long filaments spread out alive
                          like nerves
memories gradually fading.

You shred the tedium of forms
                    —voices and their finite scale,
                quadrilateral walls.

Everything predictable,
nibbled like a saddle,
            breaks its linkage.

Your voices don't retreat
            although your eye closes,
and a shout tries to frighten them off
from the field of the known.

5

Licked by an edge
            in your untroubled eyes,
the light scalds itself
on the damp stone.

In its minutest caverns,
         amid mosses and insects,
your solar pupil
halts.

Crevices in the stone,
clefts,
something that looks
                  from the depths.

Your gaze refracts
            the deep-sea landslip,
and ages of thought fall apart.

6

Clothed with the abyss,
you leave off from your step
                          on being named
your darkest brilliance.
Intoxicated,
              more than that depth.
Smooth,
              more than the night in which you envelop me.
Oh Dark one,
        oh Tremendous one,
there you hide.
When you awake, nothing is left.

And I am between my sleep
                      and your waking.
I go from my breath to your eyelid,
I am at stake
        —like the other things
        you erase
                when you open your eyes.

7

Under the cleft tree,
            door to the underworld,
something draws the heart
toward an unattained depth.

      I follow your trail.

Moss covers the evening,
ferns sprout from the fountain.
Nearby
        a cock pecks
and time hangs
          from a spider's web.

      I follow your trail
      that at mid-step
               disappears.

Sleep sinks
      in your roots.

      I look at your trail
where the tip of a leaf ends,
where endless stirring ceases.

Amid curls of fern
the trunk of the red cypress turns green again
and in those mosses of the coming summer
my death brings nearer its shores,
it duplicates your lovely mask,
              your bird silence.

I see in things your turbulent traces
and I sink in a hug
                I do not want to leave.

8

Your breeze comes covering the whole climate,
your fruit lips burn
     the mouth of winter.
Flowerings open in the skin,
    erect pistils—

Unexpected return to your hands
that brush against my sleeve,
     that approach my breast.

You overturn what you touch,
you go by dressing everything in green,
you go by leaving in coloured stains
flowers so many.

And who could
   —even knowing your power of death—
who could fulminate
that desire hidden
    in every leaf,
    in every hummingbird?

The flowery season starts
with your cumbia and your songs,
your drunk humming
   like someone expecting
     the one bound to kill him
    who lurks at every corner
      in the dark
with your tiger eyes,
your alert leap

        like someone who fears
                        in every fold
      the crouched night
with your lubricious currents,
your electric colours
          like someone who seeks
          some auspice
bee sting,
blue buzzing
          in the entrails of a bird,
an eye-tooth that bites,
        from where should it come?
a poison that ceases
only when it has invaded everything.

Eolides
Daughters of the Wind

1

They murmur your Name
                on terraces
flooded with light
facing the wine-dark sea

2

They slither in the grass
gently tangling
          their coils

hissing
    among strawflowers

3

They add their voices
to the moaning of rocks
          and bushes

They stretch the heart
            to a taut string

4

They yelp unearthly
        along the valley

They low like calves
a parched howl
an unearthly
        trilling

5

Obsessive
       like repeated scenes
of the same movie

they pound at windows
they scour endless wharves
        at dawn

6

They lash the rocks at Aghia Triada
    with its caves to hide away
        from pirates

They topple the traveler
    on the peak which is named
        Demonotopos

They lift the waves' roaring
    up to the shrine of pious chants
        to the Panaghia

7

They tousle the hair
          of the young eucalyptus
squeezing out its resins
               to fall on handrails

They buzz lovingly
like bumblebees
          in the hollow of reeds

They fill your gaze with yellow ants

8

They waken
     the guardian spirit of the olive grove
They allow the hungry animals
                    to graze patiently

They sharpen
the wasp's
     blue chisel

9

The frizzy flowers
the flank of the hills
          submit to their rhythm

They turn everything to smooth stone

10

They carry echoes
      of emphatic conversation
      of goat-bells tinkling
      of a violin

They sing at night
         airs of a Levantine lament

11

Their harped tongues
are magnified
      in the spirit's winter

They make the soul
       duck and cower
in its cranny.

12

They write your Name
with their light fingers
        in the sand

they repeat that calligraphy
        like a prayer.

from *Notebook of Amorgos*

The Islands

I

    Hamlets lost in the layers of rock. And from there, the horizon of islands, the small somnambulant lighthouse, not yet lit up.

    Under the violet dust of sunset, the immense rock, Holy Trinity, stretches its steep angles to sky and earth
                  —sudden unevenness, as in the walls of glory.

    And the sun disappears on the other side to sink into the waters, behind the uninhabited, barren islet,

    which in the morning will cut off its saurian head above the light, and in one of its ends, almost lost,
    the white, abandoned chapel will shine out,
                    —an amulet against evil spirits.

    Oh, dancing sea under the course of the seagulls, while the islands reappear, crowned with clouds.

2

    That substance opened beyond the sea, like an ant's wing on the blue breeze of the rosemary, floats omnipresent.

    Detaching from that froth of gods, it pours its glass of silence into its own solitude.

    It enters and leaves the brilliance of the waves, dissolves on the other side of conscience the last words—
                            no longer attainable in the wake of day.

    Senses sharper and sharper, they cut in their edges all the vague, profuse, dancing aura of half-sleep.

    Still heard, closing, the music of the last phrases, now lost the lyrics and the beat—

    it stays on the other side, to be found in the random cipher of the wave, in another breaking of the sea,
                              visited now by another ear.

3

The horizon is lost behind the mist.

The coastline of the islands can well be an unreal depiction, or a density of hydrogen or something non-existent,

a minimal concentration in the slate tones of the evening—a weight scarcely different from what encodes the mind of those islands.

The changing light under the pergolas, tiny grapes sprout like minutes in the cluster of days,

or purple wisterias fall on the pages of the book, desiccated words, gaze lost in its stillness, in its desire to seize a central reference,

although suddenly my gaze may confuse a buoy on the inlet with a dolphin's back, or the sun beating down with the fire of the soul.

4

All night long the song of the owls played between two notes of viola. The moon is gone paler than a cloud.

Under the east wind, the eucalyptus dances—pliant hair—flexible like a possessed woman,
                                        uncontrolled by what multiple hands dictate.

The clouds are flying away. The wind traverses the spread out beaches.

The storm would devastate the frozen palm trees, the distant explosion or the discontinuous chirping of the birds trembling on the roofs.

The wind grows in the sea and my gaze invents its own blanket of clouds, its sleepless lightness.

5

The boats have slowly docked. The cold rises where the cats timidly sniff among the heaped nets.

A violet stripe crosses the sky and my body is crossed by fine fibres of wonder and a wind that passes along my feet.

At a distance, iridescent bins are disembarked. And further off, in dream, while one tries to fix onto any point, the beach adrift,

the last images fall and are lost. What beach? Where will we run aground, like fish asleep?

All this sun with its flavour, so old that it's new, all the haste of our steps are not enough to drink

on the shoulders of a commencing autumn, the light of the bay, the ungraspable line of the islands.

6

An out-of-tune little violin came and went to open the evening, while the wind stirred the tablecloths.

The mountain was visible on the back of a cat. Among Stephanos' steps along the terrace
    the *quena* would be heard drawing all at once the Andes to the folds of Aghia Triada—

Inside, mantelpieces with photographs of the dead, faded distinction amid the sepias,
    electric candles lighting up amid flowers the long moustaches, the sabre and the rifle.

Lambs skirt the crag, and painted white, the haven against invaders shines now on high.

Ah, dance of lights filtered amid the vine and the wisteria, the clusters of violet flowers already drying, the grapes growing day after day.

7

The sun spreads out in the photograph of evening.
Thousandths of a second beat in the wing of the seagull.

Solitude collects its days under the solar pounding, distils one by one its pearls of tedium.

And following the good spirit of chance, the skin picks up the fickleness of the wind, persuasion or enchantment—

when its minatory voice exerts a false helplessness, like a cat that just gave birth. Destitute wind in the windows.

Or the sudden distance of the skin, containing the spirit of the blood, the tumult of the mind
                    —like a compass rose.

And this wind that is blowing sets white dish-cloths flying high up on a tree, or brings them trotting down the ravine.

As a wolf it howls behind the proverbial lambs, here where there are no wolves, but lambs and goats grazing on the wind,

like the vanity of things, the fickleness of the skin, desire stretching out like a cat on these Sunday sheets.

8

    The cloud leaves in its exile
                      a scandal of drops on the tiling, rises
toward the height of the neighbouring clouds.
                                    Silent cavalcades,
a brilliance on the rim of the cirrus.

    Now it fragments in flocks from gold to purple, thins its
shadow on the crag,
                    where the waves have dressed the black
rocks with algae, have opened under their pounding caves where
thoughts can graze.

    I call you and you flash in the cloud, you spread out in what
rises between the lightning and thunder.
    I call you
              and you also come to meet me.

    A sparkle, transparencies move the gaze, filter small drops of
the glimpsed torrent—
                  light like a cascade, like a deluge.

9

    Touch traverses the body, and pollen of arum visits the fingertips—
          ants on the back of the neck and in the armpit.

    Corpuscles, living essences move around in the air.
Solicitudes of light.
    The brilliance imposes its blinding edge on the perennial foliage.

    We have followed tracks under cover of the sun, and its oils nourish the hinges of the gaze,
      a current of fresh laughs, of unbroken good fortune
                      under a sun giving of thorns.

10

The scarcely perceptible lighthouse in the blotch of dawn.

To decipher dreams, as much as the many various stings of insects,
    the wind in its multiple appetencies, the whiteness of the houses behind the fig tree.

    To guess each one the speech of the other, the accents—only starting from a recognisable gesture.
    To esteem the song that dwells in us in so little life, the wine that arouses us.

    The wind bears away accumulated dream.
                                Inside, everything turns blue.
    The silhouettes gleam briefly blue and white. A cloud and seagulls, also white.

                      (The hand writes without the eyes ridding themselves of their dream).

Amorgos, Greece, 1998
Mexico City, 2003

Acknowledgements

We are grateful to Elsa Cross for permission to print the poems included in this volume. The original poems were first published in the following collections (all in Mexico City): *Bacantes* (Ediciones Artifice, 1982), *Baniano* (Editores méxicanos unidos, 1986), *Canto malabar* (Fondo de Cultura Económica, 1987), *Jaguar* (Ediciones Toledo, 1991); *Poemas desde la India* (Universidad Autónoma Metropolitana, 1993). *Urracas* (Editorial Aldus, 1996); *Cantáridas* (Ediciones sin nombre, 1999); *Los sueños — Elegías* (Conaculta, 2000), *Ultramar - Odas* (Fondo de Cultura Económica, 2002) *El vino de las cosas - Ditirambos* (Ediciones Era / Conaculta, 2004); *Cuaderno de Amorgós* (Editorial Aldus, 2007).

Ruth Fainlight's translation of 'Cantharides' was first published by Bloodaxe Books in her collection *Moon Wheels* (Bloodaxe Books, Tarset, Northumberland, 2006); we are grateful to Bloodaxe Books for permission to reprint the translation here.

John Oliver Simon's translations of 'Jaguar', 'Tenayuca', and 'Malinalco' first appeared in the anthology *Light From a Nearby Window*, ed. Juvenal Acosta (City Lights, San Francisco, 1993); together with 'Palenque' and 'In Xochicalco' these poems also previously appeared in *Bacantes y otros poemas / Translations of Light* by Elsa Cross and John Oliver Simon (Entrelíneas Editores, Mexico City, 2003).

'Magpies' previously appeared in *Shearsman* magazine.

The Translators

Anamaría Crowe Serrano lives in Dublin and translates from Italian and Spanish. Shearsman Books published her first collection of poems, *Femispheres*, in 2008.

Ruth Fainlight was born in the USA, but has lived in England since she was 15. Her first collection appeared in 1966, and her most recent, *Moon Wheels*, a collection of poems and translations, was published by Bloodaxe Books in 2006. She has also written short fiction and opera libretti, and has translated drama as well as poetry.

Luis Ingelmo lived in the United States for seven years, six of which he spent in Chicago as a teacher of Spanish. He is currently a teacher of English in Ávila, Spain. He has recently translated a volume of poems, *Native Guard* (*Guardia nativa*, Madrid, Bartleby, 2009) by the 2007 Pulitzer Prize-winner, Natasha Trethewey. He has edited volumes by Claudio Rodríguez, Juan Antonio Villacañas and Gustavo Adolfo Bécquer for Shearsman Books, and also co-translated the Rodríguez.

John Oliver Simon lives in Berkeley, California, and has published a number of collections of his own poems and many translations from Spanish, including two volumes by Elsa Cross. His most recent publications are *Translations of Light* (bilingual, translated by Elsa Cross, Entrelíneas Editores, Mexico City, 2003) and his translations of Jorge Fernández Granados, *Ghosts of the Palace of Blue Tiles* (Tameme, Inc., Los Altos, CA, 2008).

Michael Smith lives in Dublin, and has published a number of collections of his own poetry. Shearsman Books published his *Collected Poems* in 2009, and a volume of his selected translations from the Anglo-Saxon, Irish and Spanish, under the title *Maldon & Other Translations* in 2004. His translations, and co-translations, of Vallejo, Villacañas, Bécquer, Claudio Rodríguez and Rosalía de Castro have all been published by Shearsman, and others will follow. His awards include the European Academy of Poetry Medal for his services to the translation of poetry. Michael Smith lives in Dublin, and is a member of Aosdána, the Irish National Academy of Artists.